AF426208

CHEROKEE
MYTHOLOGY

A BRIEF HISTORY FROM BEGINNING TO END

HISTORY HUB

photo on right: Chris Hartford from London, UK, CC BY 2.0 Wikimedia Commons

Bonus Downloads

*Get Free Books with **<u>Any Purchase</u>** History Shorts*

Every purchase comes with a FREE download!

Cherokee Mythology

A Brief History from Beginning to the End

History Shorts

© 2022 Copyright by History Shorts. All Rights Reserved.

Please Note: The book you are about to enjoy is an analytical review meant for educational and entertainment purposes as an unofficial companion. If you have not yet read the original work, please do before purchasing this copy.

Disclaimer & Terms of Use: No part of this publication may be reproduced or retransmitted, electronic or mechanical, without the written permission of the publisher. The information in this book is meant for educational and entertainment purposes only and the publisher and author make no representations or warranties with respect to the accuracy or completeness of these contents and disclaim all warranties such as warranties of fitness for a particular purpose. Product names, logos, brands, and other trademarks featured or referred to within this publication are the property of their respective trademark holders and are not affiliated with this publication. This is an unofficial summary and analytical review meant for educational and entertainment purposes only and has not been authorized, approved, licensed, or endorsed by the original book's author or publisher and any of their licensees or affiliates.

CONTENTS

Part One: Editor Foreword

Chapter One: Introduction

Chapter Two: Location and Culture

Chapter Three: Spiritual Beliefs

Chapter Four: One With Nature

Chapter Five: Mythology

Chapter Six: Myths and Legends

Chapter Seven: Animal Mythology Examples

Chapter Eight: Changing beliefs

Chapter Nine: Modern Beliefs

Chapter Ten: Current Day Culture

Chapter Eleven: Conclusion

Chapter Twelve: Discussion Question

Chapter Thirteen: Quiz Question

Your Free Bonus Download

Chapter One
Introduction

The Cherokees are indigenous people living in the United States of America. Historically, they owned large tracts of land around modern-day Tennessee, Georgia, and Carolina. The arrival of Europeans heralded a period of displacement, war, and cultural and religious assimilation for the Cherokee Nation. The Cherokees didn't have a word for their spiritual beliefs like "religion," everything in their world had a holy significance. Cherokee myths and tales imparted the knowledge and techniques required to preserve the harmony, balance, and health of nature. Their mythological beliefs are strongly tied to their cultural practices with everyday activities like farming, hunting, storytelling, having an origin story grounded in their spiritual beliefs.

The Cherokee have two types of stories, the creation stories, and the animal tales. The creation stories are more serious in nature and included for example, the world's origin, migration, cultural "heroes" like Ka-na-ti, the first man, and Se-lu, the first woman, and the ball game played between birds and animals. These myths detail how the world came about and the role of the humans in nature, and the importance in ensuring a balance between people and the natural world. Animal tales explain why animals behave or appear a certain way and are often told as parables to provide guidance, warnings or for general amusement. The Cherokee mythological tales were shared with other Cherokee or Native American people in accordance with the old customary rule. Only those invited by the myth keeper or village storyteller would be allowed to hear the tales. Participants would need to first visit the medicine man to get ready.

Every year, the Green Corn Ceremony is held during the harvest season. This is one of the most important Cherokee ceremonies and heralds the start of a new year, the lighting of the sacred council fire, and a time when people express gratitude and ask for forgiveness. During the 1800s the Cherokees culture began to change with the adoption of colonial culture, and this was never more obvious than for their spiritual beliefs. Christian missionaries, particularly those from the Moravian Church, began to live and work amongst the Cherokee. The Cherokee were very welcoming of missionaries and did not prohibit the preaching of their religion. By 1900 many Cherokees had converted to Christianity, and this was evident in the changes made to many of their traditional ceremonies. Today, while most Cherokees identify as Christian, many have adopted a belief system that fuses traditional Cherokee beliefs with modern-day Christianity, people still dance around the everlasting fire as the men sing the melodies, and the women keep the beat. They sing and pray to the creator as they dance, which is extremely similar to the modern Christian faith. Cherokees today continue to practice in the same manner that their ancestors did, although there is a stronger affinity between Cherokee and Christian ideas.

Chapter Two
Location and Culture

The Cherokees, also known as Ani'-Yun'wiya, "the true people,"are native people who lived for hundreds of years in parts of modern-day Tennessee, Georgia, South Carolina, and North Carolina before the formation of the United States of America. They are thought to have numbered around 22,500 people in 1650 and owned 40,000 square miles (100,000 square kilometers) of the Appalachian Mountains.

The majority of the Cherokee Nation members were forced to travel the "Trail of Tears" to Oklahoma following President Andrew Jackson's Indian Removal Act of 1830. To resolve the now infamous 1835 New Echota Treaty, which resulted in the exile of the Cherokee people from the eastern United States. The last 17,000 Cherokees were forcibly marched 1,200 miles to what is now Oklahoma in 1838. Between 4,000 and 8,000 people perished along this "Trail of Tears" due to starvation, disease, and exhaustion.

However, some stayed in the mountains of North Carolina, and in 1848, Congress formally acknowledged them as the Eastern Cherokee band. Most of the 10,000 current members of the Eastern band reside on the 56,572-square-foot Qualla Boundary, close to the Great Smoky Mountains National Park. They are the only tribe in North Carolina with federal recognition and the only tribe with a reservation. In what is now Oklahoma's northeastern region, 14 counties are entirely or partially occupied by the Cherokee Nation. The United Keetoowah Band of Cherokees in Oklahoma, a second and distinct Cherokee tribal government, recognized by the federal government, is located in the same region.

Numerous organizations around the United States claim to be Cherokee bands or tribes in addition to the three Cherokee administrations recognized by the federal government. About 165,000 people are registered as citizens of the Cherokee Nation, even though the Cherokee people are currently split geographically, culturally, and politically.

Cherokee culture

When Spanish explorers discovered the Cherokee people in the middle of the 16th century, they had a wide range of stone tools, including knives, axes, and chisels. They grew corn (maize), beans, and squash, weaved baskets, and made ceramics. Meat and clothes came from elk, bear, and deer. The homes of the Cherokee were log cabins with a single door, no windows, and a smoke hole in a bark roof. In addition to a council house, where town meetings were held and a holy fire burnt, a typical Cherokee town would have between 30 and 60 similar homes. The Busk, or Green Corn Festival, commemorated the first fruits and new fires and was a significant religious ceremony. The Cherokee nation consisted of small towns and villages, a confederacy of symbolic red (for war) and white (for peace) towns. A supreme war chief oversaw the leaders of each red town, while the supreme peace chief oversaw the chiefs of each white town.

The Cherokee's adoption of American colonial culture around 1800 was notable. The tribe established a government based on the American system. They supported American President Andrew Jackson during the Creek War, particularly at the Battle of Horseshoe Bend, in his fight against the Creek. They adapted agricultural, textile, and construction techniques from this colonial era. The Cherokee language's syllabary was perhaps the most amazing example of colonial cultural adoption. It was created in 1821 by Sequoyah, a Cherokee who had fought alongside the American army in the Creek War. The syllabary, a method of writing where each sign corresponds to a syllable, was so successful that nearly the entire Cherokee tribe attained literacy.

Cherokee power peaked in the seventeenth and eighteenth centuries. Extensive family groups resided in winter and summer homes built around a ceremonial townhouse in dense, palisaded settlements. The women performed most of the labor in the fields where corn, beans, squash, and other crops were grown in the matrilineal Cherokee society. However, the Cherokee changed their way of life in response to new demands and pressure from arriving Europeans. Individual farms, nuclear families, patrilineal descent, men switching from warfare to farming (the Cherokee became an agricultural nation in the 1820s), and women learning domestic skills were now features of the Cherokee community. Around 1900, some of the eastern Cherokee's crafts were at risk of going extinct. There were fewer potters and basket weavers with the introduction of wage labor. For example, spinning and weaving decreased as more Cherokee purchased ready-made clothing. However, by the late

1920s, these crafts experienced an impressive revival as tourists from

across the USA started visiting Cherokee villages.

Chapter Three
Spiritual Beliefs

Historically Cherokees didn't have a word for their spiritual beliefs like "religion"; everything in their world had a holy significance. Their spiritual beliefs comprised their entire worldview. Cherokee myths and tales imparted the knowledge and techniques required to preserve nature's harmony, balance, and health. The moral principles of the Cherokee civilization were portrayed through songs, dances, tales, artwork, tools, and even structures.

In Cherokee ceremonies, particular numbers have significance. The numbers four and seven are frequently used in myths, rituals, and tales. The four cardinal directions, south, east, north, and west, and the known natural forces are each represented by the number four. Additionally, specific color hues are linked to these cardinal directions. In addition to being connected to directions, the number seven stands for the historical seven Cherokee clans. There are three additional directions in addition to the four cardinal ones: the Upper World, the Lower World, and the Center (the here and now). The pinnacle of holiness and purity is also symbolized by the number seven. It once had a unique significance to the Cherokee since it was believed that only the cougar and the owl could attain that level. The cougar and the owl are revered in certain versions of the Creation tale because they were the only two creatures that could sleep during all seven days of Creation. And as a result, they now have outstanding night vision and nocturnal lifestyles.

Additionally reaching this level, the pine, cedar, spruce, holly, and laurel were significant in Cherokee ceremonies. Of all, cedar is the most sacred, and its color distinguishes it from the others. The tree's wood was once used to transport the honored dead.

The Little People

The appearance of spiritual beings is also part of the Cherokee people's everyday cultural experience. Even though the spirits are distinct from people and animals, they are not regarded as "supernatural," and they fulfill an important role in the natural, physical world. Most traditional Cherokee people would encounter these supernatural beings at least once in their lives. There is a significant group of spiritual creatures called the

Little People. People cannot see them unless the spirits want them to. They look exactly like any other Cherokee when they allow themselves to be seen, except they are very little and have long hair. The Little People have several different homes, including caverns, laurel thickets, and rocky shelters. They like dancing and drumming, and they frequently assist lost children in finding their way home—not just those who are lost physically but also those who are lost morally. They are also considered to be very mischievous. Respect and extreme caution are used when dealing with the Little People. They dislike being bothered, and those who annoy them frequently end up being "puzzled" for the remainder of their lives. Therefore, when traditional Cherokee thought they could hear Little People, they would respect their privacy and not search for them. If one of the Little People was unintentionally observed or decided to reveal themselves, it was forbidden to talk about or report the incident for at least seven years. After sundown, it was customary to refrain from mentioning the Little People.

Medicine Men

Cherokees refer to the medicine men as didanawisgi. The concept of "health," which some in the modern medical professions have just recently adopted, runs through all Native American cures. Harmony between the body, mind, and spirit is referred to as health. Medicine men believe that to be healthy, people need to have a deep connection to nature and be able to create and receive harmony in all of their interactions and within themselves. Once the balance has been restored, illness and other health problems vanish. Some would view this as a cure. Cherokee custom says this is simply excellent health and a return to the body's natural state. The range of knowledge that the traditional medicine people possessed was enormous. Years of work and study went into learning the syllabary writings. Cherokee syllabary writing contains numerous formulas recorded in books ranging in size from little notebooks to huge manuscripts. The healing words used were ineffective if they were not pronounced in the Cherokee language (Tsa-la-gi ga-wo-ni-hi-s-di). The medicine men would consult their book until the words had been committed to memory. These traditional books have closely guarded writing, and anyone judged unqualified is prohibited from reading them. The spoken words are typically accompanied by physical action, like drinking a specially made beverage. For medicine people to operate at their full potential, they must be in perfect health themselves.

Witchcraft

It is significant to highlight that Cherokee witchcraft differs significantly from other cultures. Killer witches and common witches both exist in Cherokee lore. While killer witches are easily recognizable, normal witches are indistinguishable from ordinary people and therefore regarded as being more dangerous. It is considered possible for witches to trick and corrupt medicine men and force them to prescribe the wrong medication.

The Raven Mocker is one killer witch that traditional Cherokee still mentions today. The Raven Mocker is the most dreaded Cherokee witch and has a terrible spirit. Cherokee folklore claims that it robs the sick and dying of their hearts. They typically take on the appearance of old, withered men and women or become completely invisible before taking to the air in a fiery form, searching for their next prey while emitting the sounds of a raven's cry. They torture and murder their victim by cutting off their head, then swallow their victim's heart (doing so without leaving a scratch on the victim's flesh) and lengthen their life span by one year for each year that the victim would have lived. When feeding, raven mockers are generally invisible; however, those who take powerful medicine can not only see them but can also kill them. Sometimes, medicine men will

watch the dying to stop raven mockers from snatching the soul of the sick.

Chapter Four
One With Nature

Many of the Cherokee spiritual legends are associated with mountains, streams, and waterfalls that have been known for generations. The Cherokee traditionally believed that powers, dreams, visions, and signs were all gifts from the spirits. They also believe that the human and spirit worlds are interwoven, with the spirit world ruling over both. Like other indigenous peoples, the Cherokees made an effort to maintain their rightful place within nature rather than trying to dominate it. For example, a healer would inquire of a plant's spirit to learn what ailments it might be able to treat. A hunter would offer wisdom and ask for forgiveness in prayer to the ghosts of the animals they hunted. Cherokee gatherers would only take the fourth, medicinal plant they came upon, leaving the other three to grow unharmed for later use.

Each of these behaviors helped keep their world in balance. The Cherokees held that if nature's delicate equilibrium were disrupted, everyone would suffer. They were concerned that a lack of balance may result in illness, unfavorable weather, failing harvests, poor hunting, and a host of other issues. It was up to humans to maintain harmony within themselves and with other animals, plants, and people.

The Cherokee people looked to the guiding and guardian spirits of the Upper World to help maintain harmony and balance on Earth. Participating in daily prayers, rituals, and seasonal celebrations also helped keep the Earth in order.

At the new moon, before special dances, one practice known as "going to water" was carried out for people suffering from mental and physical illness. Going to the water helped to purify both the body and the spirit. The rite was carried out at dawn. A healer would lead the people to a river or brook. After entering the water, Cherokee men, women, and children would face east and submerge themselves seven times. When they came out, they would be cleansed and born anew.

The yearly Green Corn Ceremony also represented a new beginning. Every year, it is held during the harvest season. The first step was to gather and burn any leftover maize from the previous year's harvest. After that, the town's sacred council fire, lit in the prior year, was extinguished. The community then lit a new fire and expressed gratitude and forgiveness for all of their disputes and sins from the previous year (except for murder).

In the Cherokee society, women were the farmers, and they finally

presented the first of the year's new maize harvest. A feast and a new

yearly cycle began.

Chapter Five
Mythology

Our knowledge of the Cherokees is largely a result of Cherokee elders in the North Carolina Mountains granting a white man named James Mooney permission to observe and document their way of life in the 1880s. Mooney collected and recorded the Cherokee mythology in English, shedding light on the Cherokees' mythological beliefs.

Storytelling Rituals

The Cherokee mythological tales were shared with other Cherokee or Native American people in accordance with the old customary rule. Only those the myth keeper or village storyteller invited would be allowed to hear the tales. These tales included, for example, those of the world's origin, migration, cultural "heroes" like Ka-na-ti, the first man, and Se-lu, the first woman, and the ball game played between birds and animals. Participants would need first to visit the medicine man to get ready. The medicine man would scratch them as part of the ceremony. He would use a comb, typically crafted from rattlesnake teeth to scratch their arms from shoulder to elbow and elbow to the wrist. The red wounds the comb left on their arms were covered in a healing red powder. In a little dome-shaped earthen-covered tent, they could finally hear the myth keeper's tales. Until the sun appeared in the east, the stories would go on through the night and into the following morning. They would then proceed to the water. Each participant would immerse himself seven times while a priest said prayers from the water's edge.

Being a myth keeper involved many responsibilities. For these traditional tales to be told properly, these particular people needed to be actors, mimes, singers, and dancers. The Cherokee people have two kinds of storytelling: religious and animal tales. The sacred stories are serious in nature and explain how the Cherokee acquired specific healing abilities, songs, and beliefs. Animal tales explain why animals behave or appear a certain way. The animals in these tales are enormous and speak. Due to the fact they shared a common language, the Cherokee and the animals could at first converse. However, the power to communicate with animals was lost over time due to people abusing that gift by being greedy and overhunting. It is believed that a true myth keeper can change into any creature that is part of the story being told.

Chapter Six
Myths and Legends

The Creation Of The World

According to Cherokee mythology, the Earth is a massive island floating in a sea of water, suspended by a string that descends from the sky vault, which is made of solid rock and is connected to each of the four cardinal points. When the planet is old and worn out, the people will die, the strings will snap, causing the Earth to fall into the ocean, and everything will once more be covered in water.

In the beginning, everything was covered in water; the animals were above in the upper world, known as Gălûñ'lătĭ, beyond the arch. It was quite crowded, and the animals began requesting more space to live. Finally, Dâyuni'sĭ, "Beaver's Grandchild," the small water-beetle offered to go and see what it could discover after they had been pondering what was beneath the surface of the water for some time. It swam across the water's surface in all directions, yet it could not settle in one area. Then it dove to the bottom and surfaced with some soft mud, which started to spread and expand on all sides until it became the island we now know as the Earth.

Initially, the Earth was flat, incredibly supple, and damp. The animals were impatient to descend and sent out several birds to check if it was dry enough. However, the birds were unable to find a place to land and returned to Gălûñ′lătĭ. The Buzzard was sent out and instructed to make the Earth ready for them when it finally seemed the right moment. The father of every buzzard living today was the Great Buzzard. The ground was still soft as he flew low across the entire planet. Due to his extreme exhaustion, when he arrived in the land now occupied by the Cherokees, his wings started to flap and hit the ground, leaving valleys wherever they landed and mountains where they turned back up. The animals above observed this and were frightened that all the Earth would be mountains, so they called him back, but to this day, the peaks still dominate the Cherokee lands.

When the ground dried out, and the animals descended, it was still dark, so they took the sun and set it on a course to cross the island every day from east to west just overhead. However, the sun was placed too close to the Earth and the Red Crawfish, Tsiska′gĭlĭ′, had his shell burnt a bright red due to the extreme heat, spoiling his meat, which the Cherokee to this day do not consume. The sun was raised by the conjurers another handbreadth, but the temperature was still uncomfortably high. They raised it once more and then once more until it was seven handbreadths high and situated directly beneath the sky arch. This suns highest point in the sky is known as Gûlkwâ′gine Di′gălûñ′lătiyûñ′. It is seven handbreadths above the ground and is referred to as "the seventh height." The sun passes beneath this arch every day, and at night it makes its way back to the beginning point on the upper side.

Under this, there is another world that, aside from the seasons, is exactly like Earth in terms of its animals, plants, and even people. The paths that go to this underworld flow from the mountains, and the entrances are the springs at their summits. However, to travel these paths, a person must fast, go to a body of water, and have a member of the underground race serve as a guide. Because the water in the springs is constantly warmer in the winter and cooler in the summer than the outside air, it was known that the seasons in the underworld are different from Earth's.

It was unknown who created the animals and plants, but they were instructed to observe and stay awake for seven nights. They attempted to do this, and nearly all the animals were up for the first night. However, the second night saw a number of the animals fall asleep, and the third night saw even more animals fall asleep. By the seventh night, only the owl, the cougar, and a few other creatures were still awake. These were granted the ability to see, move around in the dark, and hunt down birds and other animals that must sleep at night. Of the plants, only the cedar, pine, spruce, holly, and laurel trees were awake until the very end. To them, it was given the ability always to remain green and provide the best medicine, but to the rest, it was said: "Because you have not persevered to the end, you shall lose your hair every winter."

After the Creation of animals and plants, men followed. Initially, there was only a man and a woman. They argued before he hit her with a fish and instructed her to multiply. She gave birth to a child in seven days, then another every seven day after that. The number of people grew quickly to the point where the planet might not have been able to support them all at the rate of growth. It was thus decided that a woman is only allowed to have one child per year.

Kanáti and Selu were two of the first people born. Their names are The Lucky Hunter and Corn, respectively. Kanáti would go hunting and bring home an animal for Selu to cook. When Kanáti and Selu had a child, that child made friends with another boy who had been made from the blood of the dead animals. The family treated the boy as one of their own, although they called him "The Wild Boy." One day, the boys decided to follow Kanáti in secret after noticing that he frequently returned home with animals from his hunting trips. They followed Kanáti to a large boulder. They observed that when Kanáti moved the boulder, which concealed a cave, an animal would emerge from the cave only to be slain by Kanáti. After some time, the boys returned to the boulder alone and, in secrecy, opened the cave's entrance. Before the boys could react, numerous animals escaped through the cave's mouth. When Kanáti spotted the animals, he understood what must have happened. He set off for the cave and found that all the animals and birds had escaped. Kanáti was furious with the boys. Since that day, people have had to search for animals to hunt.

The boys returned home hungry and exhausted, asking Selu for some food. Selu told them there was no meat but to wait at the house while she got some food from the storehouse nearby. The boys wondered how she always managed to bring back baskets of maize and beans when the storehouse was so small. They decided to ignore her instructions to wait for her and followed her instead. They learned Selu's trick: to stroke her flanks and stomach to fill baskets with beans and maize. The boys realized their mother was a witch trying to poison them and must be killed. Making the boy's dinner, Selu realized her secret had been discovered. The boys killed their mother but not before Selu explained how they could continue growing crops in her absence. If the boys dragged Selu's body seven times in a circle and then seven times over the dirt in the circle, a field of corn would appear the following morning if they stayed up all night to observe. The boys neglected to follow the instructions exactly, and as a result, today, maize can only grow in specific locations on Earth and does not grow immediately.

Cherokee Gods

The Great Spirit, Unetlanvhi "Creator," who rules over all and made the Earth, is revered by the Cherokee. It is believed that the Unetlanvhi is omnipotent, omniscient, and omnipresent. It is also supposed to have created the world to provide for its offspring and to have power comparable to that of Dâyuni's, the Water Beetle. The Wahnenauhi Manuscript adds that God is also known as Kalvlvtiahi (the "Maker of All Things") and Unahlahnauhi ("The One Who Lives Above"). The Great Spirit is rarely personified as having human traits or taking on a physical human form in most oral and written Cherokee theologies.

The Red Man or Woman is called upon in spells to heal the sick as Asgaya Gigagei. Depending on the patient's gender, Asgaya Gigagei is either male or female.

"The Lucky Hunter" is Kanati, referred to as First Man. He resides in the east, where the sun rises, with his wife Selu "Corn," while their kids, the Twin Thunder Boys, reside in the west.

Ocasta "Stonecoat" the term refers to his flint piece coat, from which it derives. Ocasta was one of the helpers of the Creator, equally benign and bad. As he wandered from town to hamlet, sowing discord, Ocasta made witches. Ocasta was impaled with a stick driven through his heart by a group of women who had trapped him. The men burned Ocasta at the stake, who taught them songs and dances for hunting, warfare, and healing while he burned on his funeral pyre. Some of the men present received extraordinary powers and started the tradition of medicine men.

The Thunder Beings

According to Cherokee legend, the Great Thunder and his two Thunder Boys sons reside in the western part of the sky vault. They wear rainbows and lightning as clothing. The thunder comes to the people after the priests have prayed to him, bringing rain and blessings from the south. People were often thought to be harmed by thunder beings who resided near the Earth's surface in cliffs, mountains, and waterfalls, and this did occur. These other thunder beings are considered to be dangerous and should be avoided.

Disease and Medicine

It is believed that all living things, plants, animals, and people, once coexisted peacefully with no division between them. Up until the point where people became more powerful, the animals were bigger and stronger. Animals lost their superior strength when human numbers and weaponry both grew. The animals decided to convene a conference to consider what steps needed to be taken for their safety. First, to gather, the bears decided to create their own weapons, just like the humans, which created more confusion. Following a meeting to deliberate their course of action, the deer decided that if a hunter were to kill a deer, the hunter would contract a disease. Asking the spirit of the deer for forgiveness was the only way to ward off this illness. The people also can only kill when absolutely necessary. Next, the council of birds, insects, and small animals got together and determined that because humans were so greedy, they should infect them with various diseases. The plants learned what the animals were plotting, and because they had always been nice to people, they swore to develop a treatment for any ailment the animals could devise. Since then, plants have provided medicine to people, with each plant having a specific purpose. A medicine man will consult a plant's spirit to give guidance on which remedy to apply for each patient's illness.

The Origin of Fire

In everyday life, fire is an extremely useful instrument. The Cherokee relate a myth about the origin of fire.

Long ago, when the Earth began, there was no fire, and it was very cold. Then the above-world inhabitants, known as the Thunders, sent lightning to ignite a huge, hollow sycamore tree growing on an island. The smoke was visible to all animals, but they were unsure how to approach the fire. To decide what to do, they all gathered. They started by sending the Raven, a capable flier who would undoubtedly succeed. After landing on the sycamore tree, Raven's feathers turned black from the heat, and he took off without setting anything on fire.

Then, Screech Owl flew by. However, when he peered down the hollow trunk, a powerful blast of hot air almost burned out his eyes; they remain red to this day. Both Horned Owl and Hoot Owl tried but were unsuccessful. The animals sent snakes, but they suffocated from the smoke before they could get close to the fire. The other animals could only think of reasons not to go because they were terrified. Little Water Spider finally decided to try. Although the other animals were aware of her speed on the water, they didn't think she could bring any fire back. She remarked, "I'll manage ."To reach the island and its flaming tree, Water Spider first spun her thread into a little bowl on her back before crossing the water. She plucked a tiny piece of coal from the fire and put it in her basket. Then she returned to the other animals gliding across the water. Since then, the Earth has had fire.

The Return of Tobacco

When the world began, when all living things were one, there was only one tobacco plant, and everyone flocked to it for their tobacco until the Dagûlkû geese stole it and carried it to the south. Without it, the populace was in pain, and one elderly woman became so frail that everyone predicted her impending death unless she could obtain tobacco to prolong her life. The little mole tried to get there by tunneling under the ground, but the Dagûlkû observed his trail and murdered him as he emerged.

The Hummingbird finally offered to retrieve the tobacco, but the others declined, saying he was far too little and should probably stay home. After pleading with them to let him attempt, they took him to a plant in a field and instructed him to let them see his method. They spotted him seated on the plant before he vanished the next second, and then, due to his quick movements, neither they nor anybody else could witness him leave or return. "This is the method I'll use." said the Hummingbird, and the others were impressed.

He took off toward the east and found the tobacco plant, the Dagûlkû were watching it from all sides, but they were unable to notice him because of his small size and rapid flight. Before the Dagûlkû realized what had happened, he dashed down to the plant—tsa!—and snatched off the top of the plant comprising the leaves and seeds. The elderly woman had fainted before he arrived home with the tobacco, and they had assumed she was dead. However, when she inhaled the smoke, she opened her eyes and came back to life with a shout of "Tsâ′lû! [Tobacco!]".

The Milky Way

Some folks in the south used a corn mill to grind the corn into meal, and on a few occasions, when they went to fill it in the morning, they discovered that some of the meal had been taken overnight. When they searched the ground and found dog tracks, they decided to keep an eye on it the following night. When the dog came in from the north and started eating from the bowl, they sprang out and beat him. The meal dropped from his jaws as he raced away, and he howled off to his home in the north, leaving behind a white path that the Cherokee now refer to as "Where the dog ran," or where today we can see the Milky Way.

The Great Deluge

In the distant past, a man owned a dog that started to regularly visit the river to gaze at the water and howl. When the man finally lost his temper and reprimanded the dog, the dog replied, "There is going to be a great torrent, and the water will be so high that everyone will drown, but if you make a raft, you can be saved, but you must first throw me into the water. If you want to see proof that I'm telling the truth, check the back of my neck," the dog advised the man, who did not believe it. He turned to look and noticed that the dog's neck had the skin peeled off, leaving the bones exposed.

He started to construct a raft after coming to believe the dog. Soon it began to rain, so he gathered his family and set out with lots of supplies. Long periods of rain caused the flood to rise, covering the mountains and killing all living things on Earth. Once the rain stopped and the waters started to recede, it was finally safe to leave the raft. The father and his family were the only ones still living at the time, but one day they heard dancing and shouting coming from the opposite side of the mountain slope. The man ascended to the top and peered down; all was calm, but he noticed huge piles of bones from people and animals that had drowned all over the valley, and that's when he realized that spirits had been dancing

there.

Chapter Seven
Animal Mythology Examples

The Rabbit Dines The Bear

The bear requested that the Rabbit join him for dinner. Although they had beans in the pot, there wasn't enough fat to cook them in, so the bear cut a hole in his side and let the oil drain until there was enough to cook the meal. "That's a useful technique," the Rabbit said as he looked shocked. "I intend to attempt that."Four days later, when he returned home, he invited the bear to join him for dinner.

The Rabbit announced, "I have beans for dinner, too," as the bear arrived. I'll get the grease for them right away. He stabbed himself in the side with a knife, but blood flowed out instead of oil, and he collapsed almost instantly. After picking him up, the bear laboriously tied the wound shut and stopped the flow of blood. "You little fool, I'm enormous and powerful and lined with fat all over; the knife doesn't hurt me, but you're small and slender, and you can't do such things," he said as a reprimand.

How The Deer Got Its Horns

The deer's head was initially smooth, just like a doe's, and he had no horns. The deer was a terrific runner, while the Rabbit was an excellent jumper, and the animals were curious to see who could run or jump farther in the same amount of time. After much discussion, they finally set up a contest between the two and made a nice, big pair of antlers to reward the victor. The one who emerged from the thicket first would receive the horns. They were instructed to begin from one side of the thicket and proceed through it together before turning around and returning.

On the scheduled day, every animal was present, and antler markers were placed at the thicket's edge to indicate where to start. "I don't know this part of the country; I want to take a peek through the bushes to see where I am to run," the Rabbit said as everyone gazed at the horns. They agreed it was fine, so the Rabbit entered the bush. However, he was gone for so long that the animals eventually realized he must be up to one of his tricks. They dispatched a messenger to search for him, and out in the thicket, he saw the Rabbit eating down the bushes and yanking them out of the path until he had a road cleared to the other side.

The messenger turned around and went back to inform the other animals. They accused the Rabbit of cheating when he emerged, but he denied it until they entered the bush and discovered the open path. As they all agreed that a cheat like him had no business competing, they handed the horns to the deer, who was acknowledged to be the best runner, and he had worn them ever since. They advised the Rabbit that since he loved to remove bushes, he might make a fortune doing that hereafter, and he still does it today.

The Smelly Mink

The mink was such a master thief that the animals eventually called a council to discuss the situation. They caught the mink, constructed a massive fire, and then threw him into it after deciding to burn him to teach him a lesson. After a time, they took him out of the fire as the flames grew, and they could smell cooked flesh. They decided he had received sufficient punishment and would probably behave better going forward. The mink was scorched black by his punishment and has remained black ever since. He also still smells like roasted meat when being attacked or excited. The lesson did not last long, and today the mink remain one of the greatest thieves.

Animal Migration

There was once a great famine in the mountains. All the animals and birds that lived there came together and sent the pigeon to see if any food could be found in the low country. This time was back when the animals used to talk and hold councils, and the grubworm and woodchuck used to marry people. After some while, she returned and said she had discovered a nation where the food was "up to our ankles" above the ground. So they formed an army and marched down into the lowlands.

The Gobbling Turkey

The grouse used to have a beautiful voice and a fantastic ball play halloo. All the animals and birds played ball back then, and they were just as proud of a loud halloo as today's ball players are. Because the turkey's voice wasn't very good, he asked the grouse to tutor him. The turkey promised to provide him with some feathers so he could create himself a collar, and the grouse agreed to instruct him. The grouse's collar made of turkey feathers came about in this way. The lessons began, and the turkey progressed quickly until the grouse decided it was time to try his voice. The grouse continued, "Now, I'll stand on this hollow log, and when I tap on it to signal, you must halloo as loudly as you can." As a result, he climbed up on the log and prepared to tap on it as a grouse would. However, when he gave the signal, the turkey was so thrilled and anxious that he could not shout, just gobbling instead. Since that day, he has gobbled anytime he hears a disturbance.

Are You Enjoying Reading?

As an independent publisher

with a tiny marketing budget

we rely on readers, like you.

If you're receiving help from this book,

would you please take a moment to write a brief review?

We really appreciate it.

Chapter Eight
Changing Beliefs

Section 1 The Spread of Christianity

Early explorers, settlers, and missionaries did not recognize native beliefs as a religion since they were so dissimilar from the Christian faith of the Europeans. For instance, the white Christians did not understand the religious significance of "going to water," thanksgiving celebrations, or practices for keeping balance. These local customs appeared to the Christian Europeans, who typically saw the Native Americans as "savage heathens" to be childlike magic and superstition.

To have more area for white settlement, the Europeans had almost immediately tried to persuade the locals to give up their long-established tribal hunting grounds. Following the Revolutionary War (1776–1783), the American government started formulating a "civilization" policy to pacify and convert the Native Americans to Christianity.

As European settlers moved westward in the 1700s, the Cherokee culture, once spread over thousands of miles in the Southeast, started changing drastically. Christian missionaries, particularly those from the Moravian Church, began to live and work amongst the Cherokee. The Cherokee were welcoming of missionaries and did not prohibit preaching their beliefs. Before the American Revolution, the first Cherokee were converted to Christianity, and by the early 1800s, many well-known figures were ardent believers.

Section 2 Cherokee Conversion to Christianity

The Cherokees had long permitted several Christian denominations to start missions in their territory. Many Cherokees converted to Christianity to comprehend the world of the white man, and many were anxious to learn English and other skills from the missionaries. They believed that if they could read and comprehend white documents, they would be better able to thwart white settlers' attempts to annex their tribal lands.

The Christian bible's New Testament was eventually translated into Cherokee and written in the language's syllabary. Cherokee-language hymns, services, and scriptures started to appear. Nevertheless, communities incorporated more traditional Cherokee virtues like sharing and respect into the rituals of their brand-new Christian churches. Even some of the conventional Cherokee healers rose to the position of elder or minister in Christian congregations. Religious writing, particularly translations from the Christian Scriptures, flourished with the adoption of a written constitution. The Cherokee Phoenix, the first newspaper for Native Americans, debuted in February 1828. Today the majority of Cherokee identify as Christion. However, there are still remnants of traditional beliefs in the use of native plants for healing, in dances that emphasize Cherokee identity, in references to some of the earliest sacred Cherokee sites, and in an annual festival that occurs during the Green Corn season.

Chapter Nine
Modern Beliefs

Section 1 The Amalgamation Of Christianity With Traditional Beliefs

The Green Corn Ceremony and other traditional ceremonies were still practiced by some eastern Cherokee in 1900, although they had been altered and were no longer as common. The religious overtones in Cherokee dance and theatre have allegedly been lost and reduced to little more than creative traditions. Cherokees made up an ever-growing majority of churchgoers in 1900, but the sermons were delivered in the Cherokee language, and the religious rituals heavily included aspects of traditional cosmology, resulting in hybrid religion. On the Qualla Boundary reservation in North Carolina, there were ten churches by 1913, and all but two of them had Cherokee preachers who delivered sermons in their language. Some of these preachers were traditional medicine men and ceremonial leaders who saw no conflict between traditional religion and Christian teachings. Christian prayers were always said before council meetings.

Today the traditional religion is no longer practiced by many Cherokee. Many are devout Christians who view the traditional methods as "pagan." While others still follow the traditional beliefs in conjunction with Christianity fusing Christian doctrine with elements of Cherokee tradition.

Section 2 Similarities Between Cherokee Traditional Beliefs And Christianity

Despite their evident differences, the two "religions" have certain similarities. For instance, Christian baptisms are similar to the Cherokee "going to the water ceremony" and are both seen as important initiation processes into the faith. Then there is Stone Coat, the main character in Cherokee mythology, who gave his life for his people and is considered a Christ-like figure in Cherokee culture.

From the Creation tales, it is clear that many important Cherokee religious practices and beliefs share striking similarities with those of early modern Catholic and Protestant Europeans. These societies, too, credited a creation tale (as described in Genesis), revered a Creator God, feared a cunning subordinate god (Lucifer), and anticipated that each person's soul would live forever in a hereafter that was superior to the here and now in every way. They, too, worshipped their deity with prayers and offerings, and a highly educated clergy supported their society during times of adversity. Last but not least, most early modern Europeans worried about witches and wondered what their dreams meant.

Section 3 Differences Between Cherokee Traditional Beliefs And Christianity

Significant differences should not be overlooked as important as it is to recognize the similarities between the religious traditions of early modern Europeans (and Euro-Americans) and Native Americans. The fact that the Cherokees did not discriminate between the supernatural and the natural is the most important. Cherokees saw the "physical" and "spiritual" as being in a single, interconnected reality. According to Cherokee beliefs, their strong relationships with "guardian spirits," a wide variety of "supernatural" beings who gave their natural kin life and power, allowed plants, animals, and humans to become divine. Contrarily, Protestant and Catholic traditions tend to emphasize the distance between sinful humans

Chapter Ten
Current Day Culture

Although the majority of Cherokee today identify as Christian, representing several different denominations, they continue to practice traditional beliefs. The rhythms and beauty of the old folktales are still present in Cherokee storytelling traditions, even though most tales are now recounted in English. Grandparents share stories with children in their homes and communities, and some storytellers perform for national audiences. Cherokee stories use the exploits of characters like possums, turtles, deer, and others to teach youngsters and remind adults what it means to be a Cherokee. To completely comprehend witchcraft among the Cherokee, one must grasp that witchcraft, conjuring, and the use of medicine have persisted as essential elements of Cherokee society even today.

Originally, dancing, welcoming guests, wooing, and ceremonies all used Cherokee music. The instruments used were water drums, gourd rattles, turtle shell rattles, and rivercane flutes. Unanimous singing or call-and-response singing was used for dancing. In the dance traditions, a male leader would sing the melodies while also shaking or drumming. Women contributed vital rhythms by dancing while sporting turtle shell rattles connected to their knees. The Cherokees developed a vibrant heritage of instrumental music once the fiddle was introduced to them in the eighteenth century. At this point, Christian songs started to appear in Cherokee music. Cherokee people still practice their ancient, sacred dancing and singing customs today. They also sing gospel songs and hymns in Cherokee and English, frequently in three-part harmony and with guitar accompaniment.

Today, the Cherokee people still dance around the everlasting fire as the men sing the melodies, and the women keep the beat. They sing and pray to the Creator as they dance, which is extremely similar to the modern Christian faith. Cherokees today continue to practice the same way their ancestors did, although there is a stronger affinity between Cherokee and Christian ideas. Today, many Cherokees attend and belong to churches, including Methodist, Presbyterian, Unitarian, and others. A sizable number of Cherokee Baptists are found among the more traditional Cherokees. Cherokee Baptists gather in what is known as "Indian churches," where they sing hymns and read the New Testament in Cherokee. The Cherokee language is used for the services. The Cherokee Baptist church has been credited with saving the Cherokee language from extinction. While the claim is debatable, there is no denying the church's importance in maintaining the Cherokee language. When Cherokees discuss "traditional people," they frequently refer to Cherokee Baptists.

The Eastern Cherokee tribe still practices their music, storytelling, dance, food-making, basket-making, headwork, pottery, blowgun-making, flint-knapping, and other cultural traditions today. Their language is being reintroduced in classrooms and society after being banned by federal schools for more than 50 years. The foundation of Cherokee culture is a desire for world peace and balance. Being in balance entails taking responsibility for one's actions and keeping in mind the welfare of those involved, including the family, tribe, and nature.

Every year thousands of tourists flock to the Cherokee Nation to experience an indigenous people's culture firsthand. Today you can visit the many museums highlighting the Cherokee's history and modern-day cultural beliefs. People can enjoy outdoor activities such as hiking, fishing, and boating at Natural Falls State and Tenkiller State Parks. The Cherokee people run dozens of restaurants and cafes, providing a unique culinary

experience serving traditional foods prepared as they were hundreds of

years ago.

Chapter Eleven
Conclusion

The mythology of the Cherokee people is a rich tapestry of beliefs involving a physical world deeply interwoven with a spiritual one. People look to the spirits, gods, animals and birds for guidance. This has led to a strong sense of place within nature, where maintaining harmony between man and nature is key to the Earth's survival. The Cherokee firmly believe that disrupting this delicate balance can have disastrous consequences for mankind. These beliefs became strongly linked to their cultural identity and were evident in everyday life, from storytelling to traditional ceremonies, hunting, farming, and the practice of healing by medicine men. The arrival of Europeans changed the fabric of Cherokee culture forever and the arrival of Christian missionaries led to many Cherokee converting to Christianity over a short period of time.

Although the majority of Cherokee today identify as Christian, representing several different denominations, they continue to practice traditional beliefs. The rhythms and beauty of the old folktales are still present in Cherokee storytelling traditions, even though most tales are now recounted in English. Grandparents share stories with children in their homes and communities, and some storytellers perform for audiences across the nation. Cherokee stories use the exploits of characters like possums, turtles, deer, and others to teach youngsters and remind adults what it means to be a Cherokee.

The last few decades have seen a revival of traditional Cherokee practices. With more and more people practicing traditional music, storytelling, dance, flint-knapping, food-making, beadwork, pottery, and other cultural traditions today. The Cherokee language is being reintroduced into classrooms after being banned by federal schools for over 50 years. The foundation of Cherokee culture remains strong, a desire for peace and balance, taking responsibility for one's actions and being mindful of the welfare of the family, the tribe and the natural world.

Chapter Twelve

Discussion Question

The Cherokee people took most of their myths and legends from nature.

This is true of many indigenous cultures. Why do you think this is?

Discussion Question

The beliefs of the Cherokee people had many similarities to Christianity.

List them. Discuss their similarities.

Discussion Question

Explain the importance of storytelling in the Cherokee culture. What other means did the Cherokee use to disseminate stories? Which do you think would have been more effective? Justify your answer

Discussion Question

How did the Cherokee treat Christian missionaries? Explain their attitude. Has history shown that it was the right attitude for them to have?

Discussion Question

What differences exist between Cherokee and Christian religions? The Cherokees did not distinguish between the supernatural and the natural world. How is this a significant difference?

Discussion Question

Which is your favorite Cherokee myth? Explain your choice. What similarities are there between the Cherokee Creation story and the Christian Biblical Creation Story?

Discussion Question

Who was Stonecoat? Do you think the Christian missionaries might have

had a problem with that character? Yes or no? Explain your answer.

Discussion Question

How has Cherokee culture survived? What laws and acts were put in
place to ensure their survival? Do you think they have been effective?

Chapter Thirteen
Quiz Question

1. **True/False:** According to the Cherokees, the mountains were formed by the Great Bald Eagle. It made valleys and mountains in the soft earth. Unfortunately, it failed to make sufficient valleys.

2. **True or False.** The Christian bible's New Testament was translated into Cherokee. It was written in the syllabary of the Cherokee language. Cherokee-language hymns, services, and scriptures started to appear.

3. **True/False:** The bear cooked beans by stabbing himself in the side and allowing fat to pour into the pot. When the rabbit tried that, he nearly bled to death. That's because he was too thin.

4. **True/False:** The water spider carried a bowl on her back before crossing the water. She plucked a tiny piece of coal and put it in her basket. Then she returned to the other animals, but the rabbit stole it and took the credit.

5. **True/False:** After the Revolutionary War (1776–1783), the American government decided to develop a "civilization" policy. This was intended to pacify and convert the Native Americans to Christianity. This was largely effective.

6. **True/ False:** The Cherokees were unwilling to let missionaries preach in their land. They regularly executed missionaries who strayed onto their territory. This was not well received in Washington (False. The missionaries were well received.)

7. **True/False:** Our understanding of Cherokees' way of life is a result of Cherokee elders in the North Carolina Mountains giving a white man permission to document their way of life. James Mooney in the 1880s was the man who did this. He collected and recorded their myths in English.

8. **True/False:** Cherokees believed that a healthy mind equaled a healthy body. They believed in holism. They felt that unity of body, mind and spirit would take them down the path to health.

Quiz Answer

1. False. It was the Great Buzzard, the father of all living buzzards today, who in his exhaustion created mountains and valleys as his wings brushed the surface of the earth.

2. True

3. True

4. False. The water spider brought fire to the animals, the rabbit did not steal the coal and claim the credit for bringing fire to the animals.

5. True

6. False. The missionaries were well received by the Cherokee people who allowed them to preach in their lands and began converting Cherokees to Christianity.

7. True

8. True

Bonus Downloads

*Get Free Books with **<u>Any Purchase</u>** History Shorts*

Every purchase comes with a FREE download!

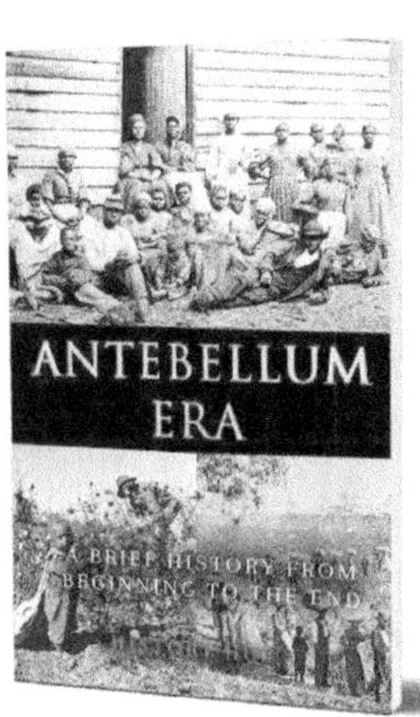

Thank You For Reading

As an independent publisher

with a tiny marketing budget

we rely on readers, like you.

If you're receiving help from this book,

would you please take a moment to write a brief review?

We really appreciate it.

www.ingramcontent.com/pod-product-compliance
Lightning Source LLC
Chambersburg PA
CBHW080942120726
48003CB00011B/3267